Sexy Art: Guide To Drawing Erotic Manga

Mature Art: Erotic Manga Drawing Lessons

How to Draw Erotic Manga

By: Gala Publication

2

Published By:

Gala Publication
ISBN-13: **978-1522802389**
ISBN-10: **152280238X**

©Copyright 2015 – Gala Publication

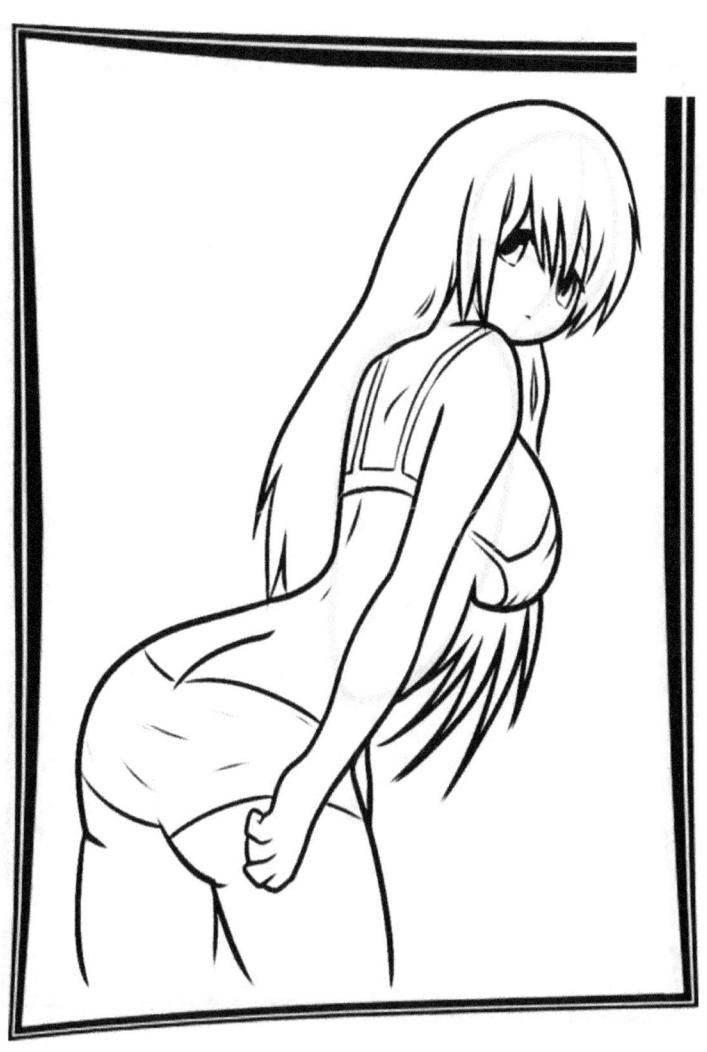

Character 1

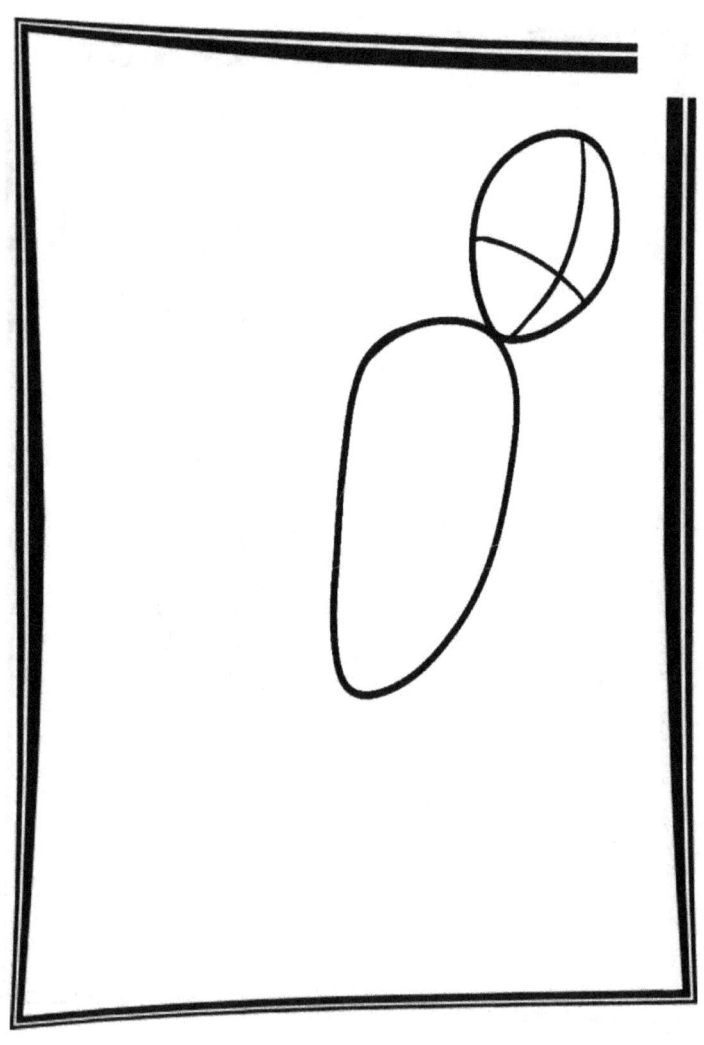

STEP 1

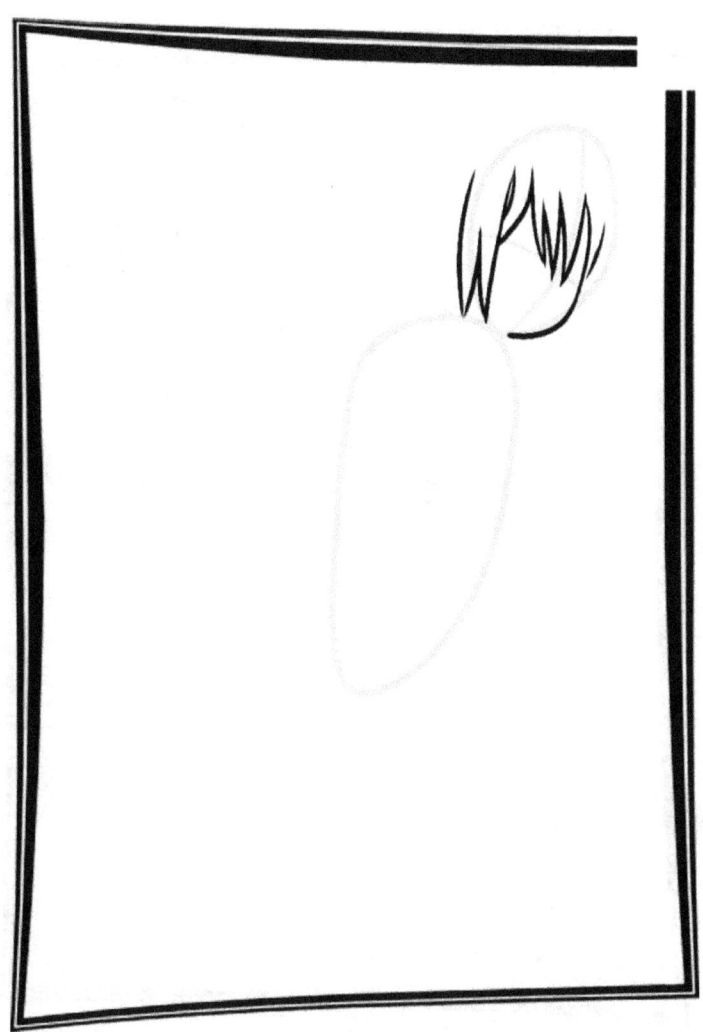

STEP 2

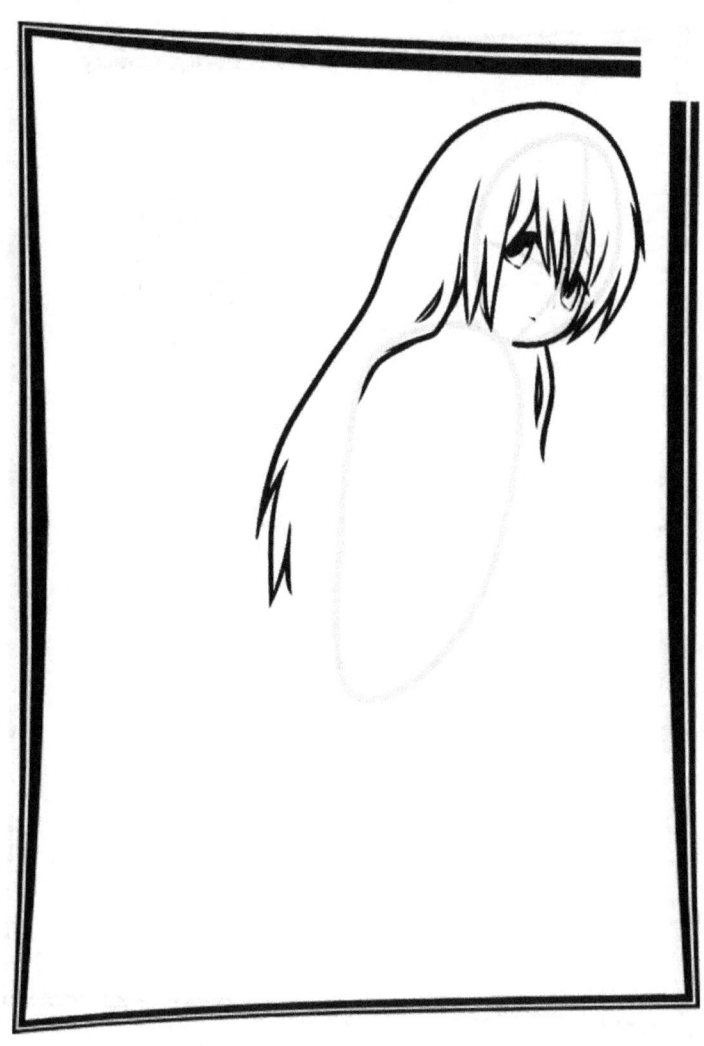

STEP 3

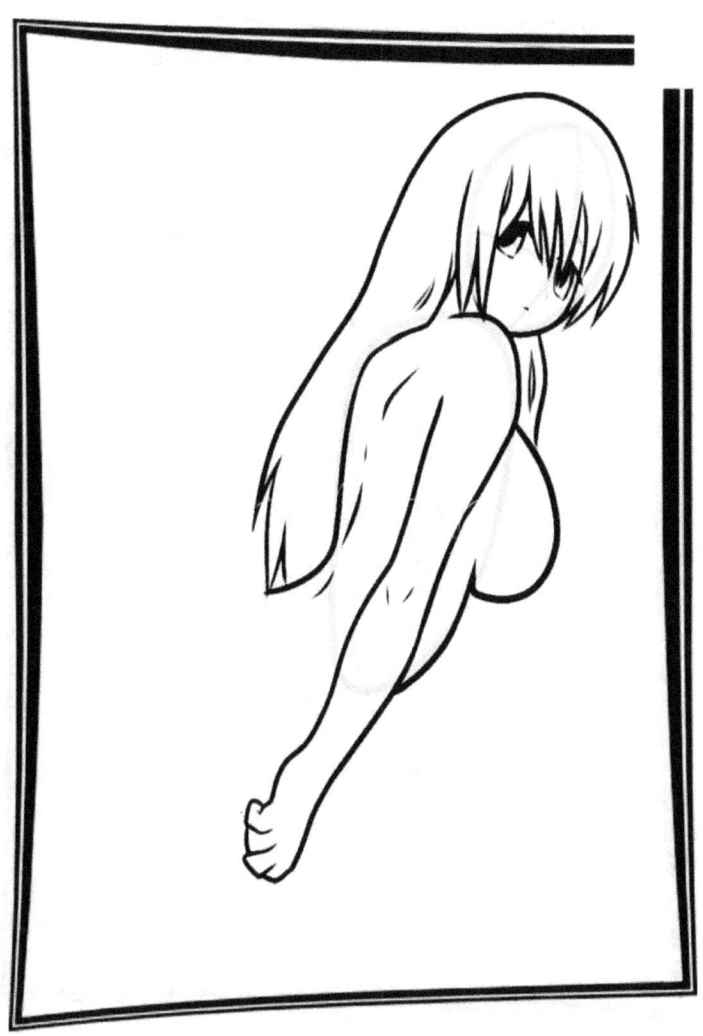

STEP 4

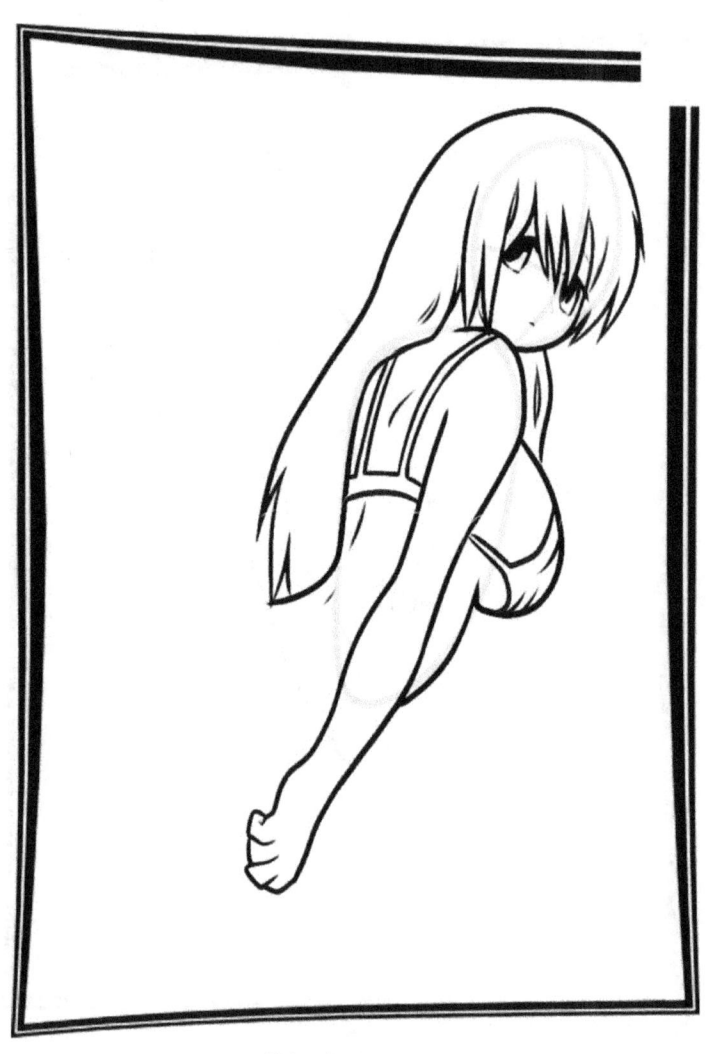

STEP 5

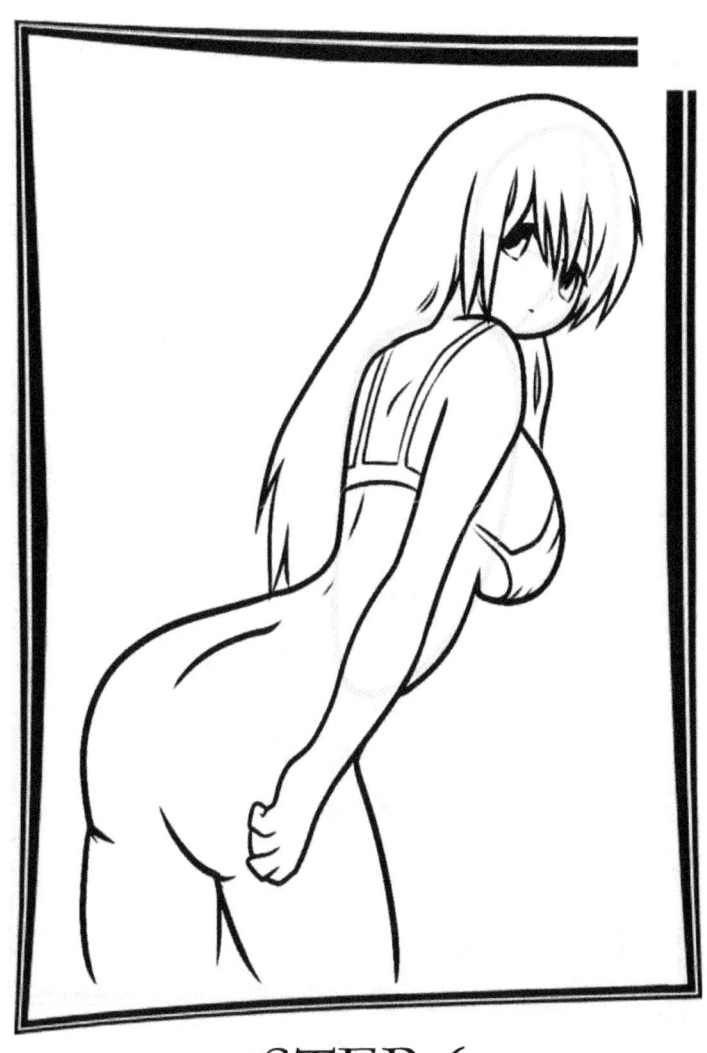

STEP 6

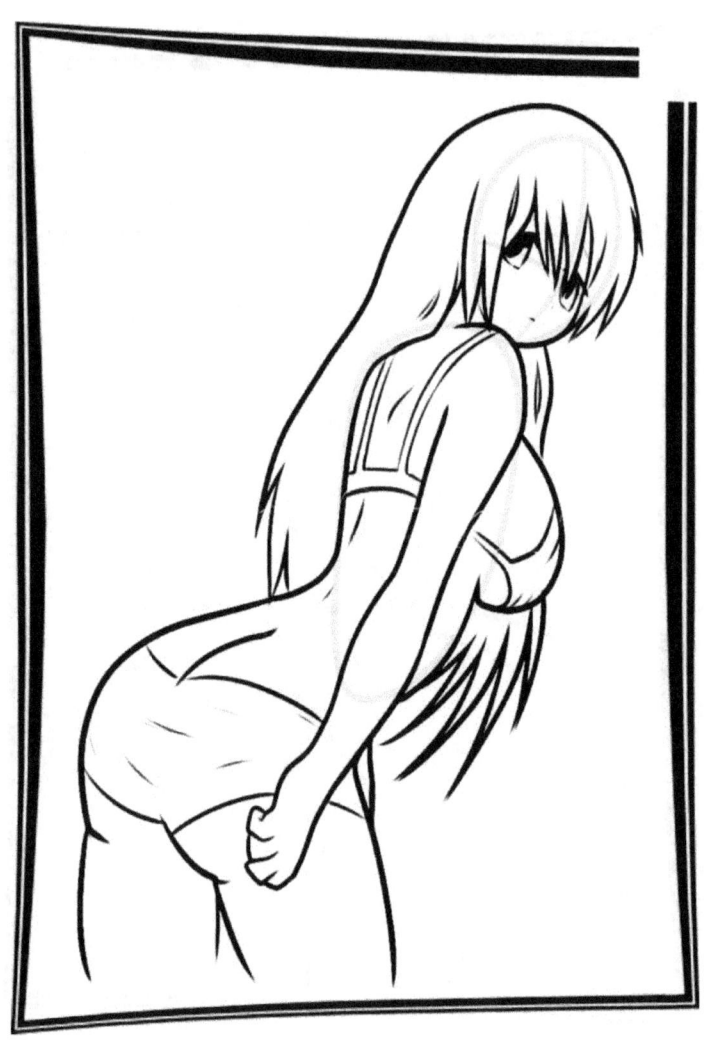

STEP 7

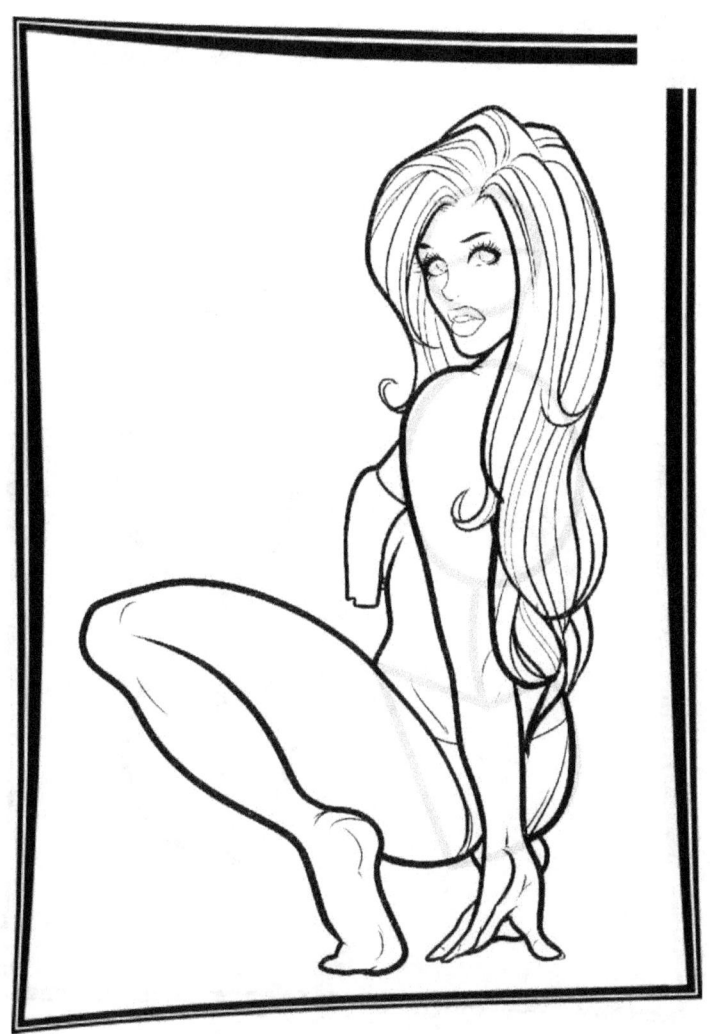

Character 2

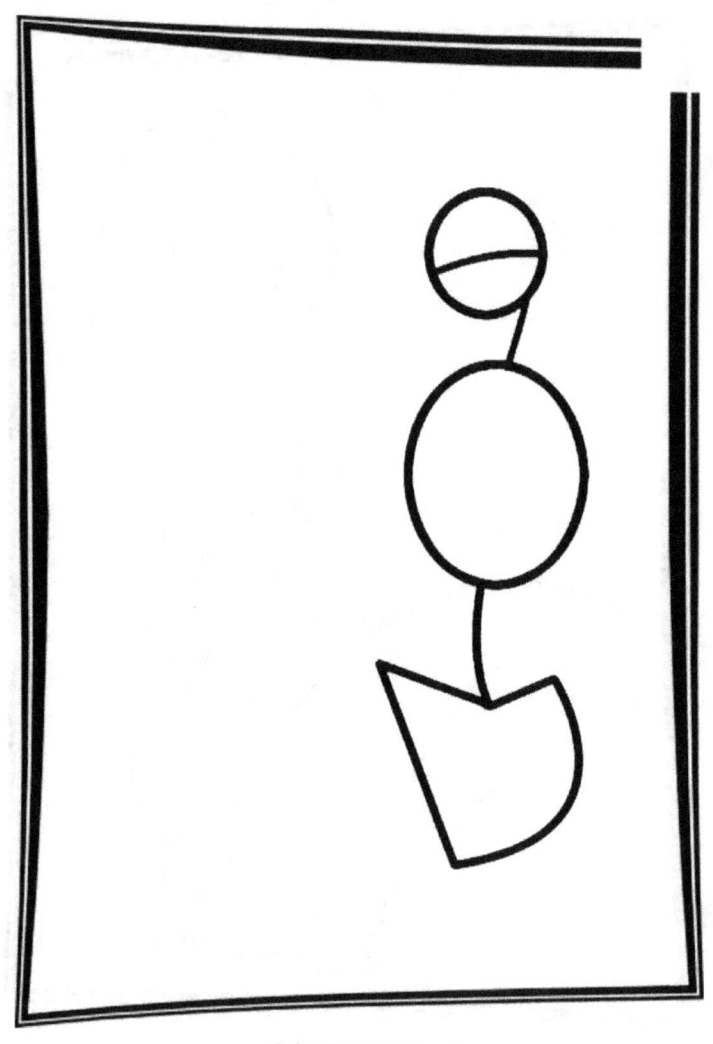

STEP 1

13

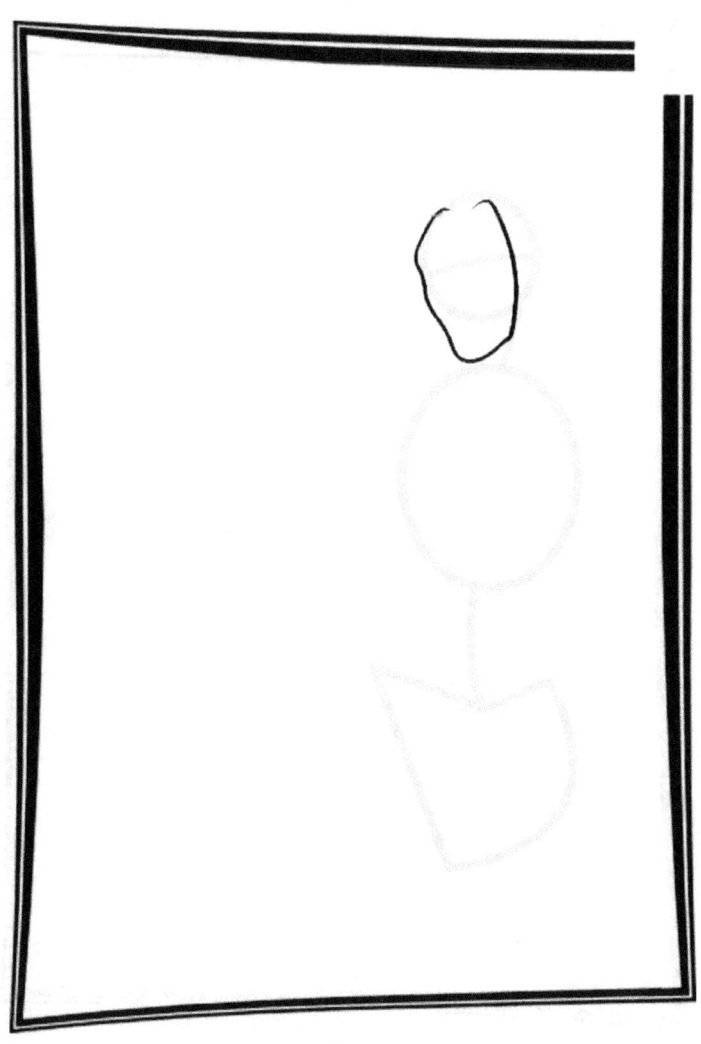

STEP 2

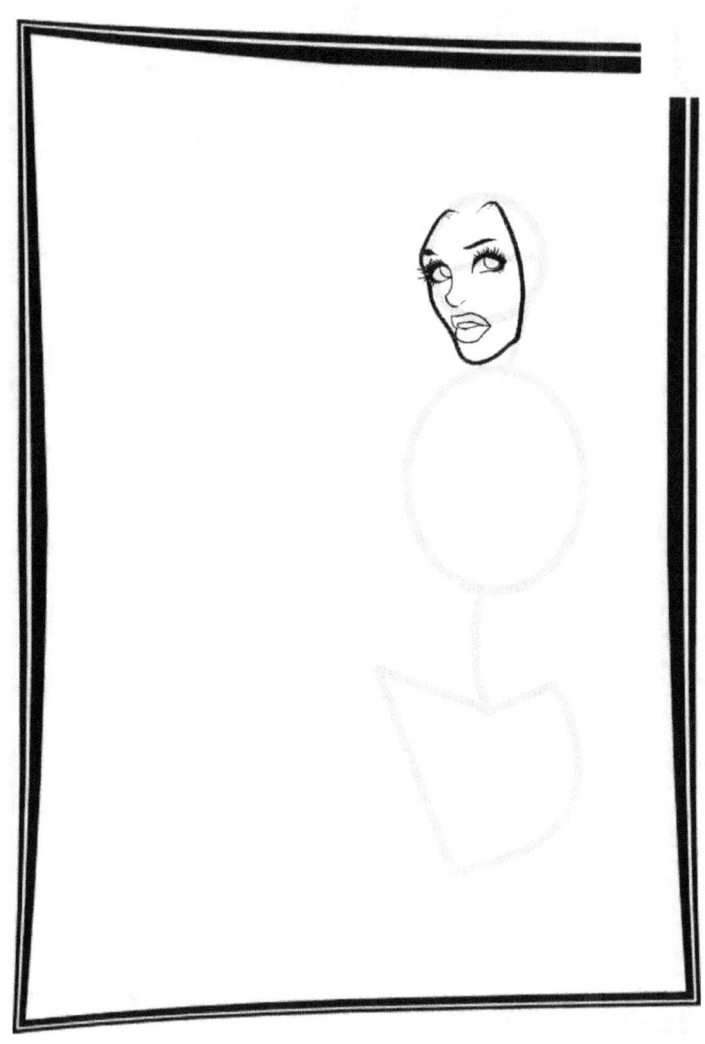

STEP 3

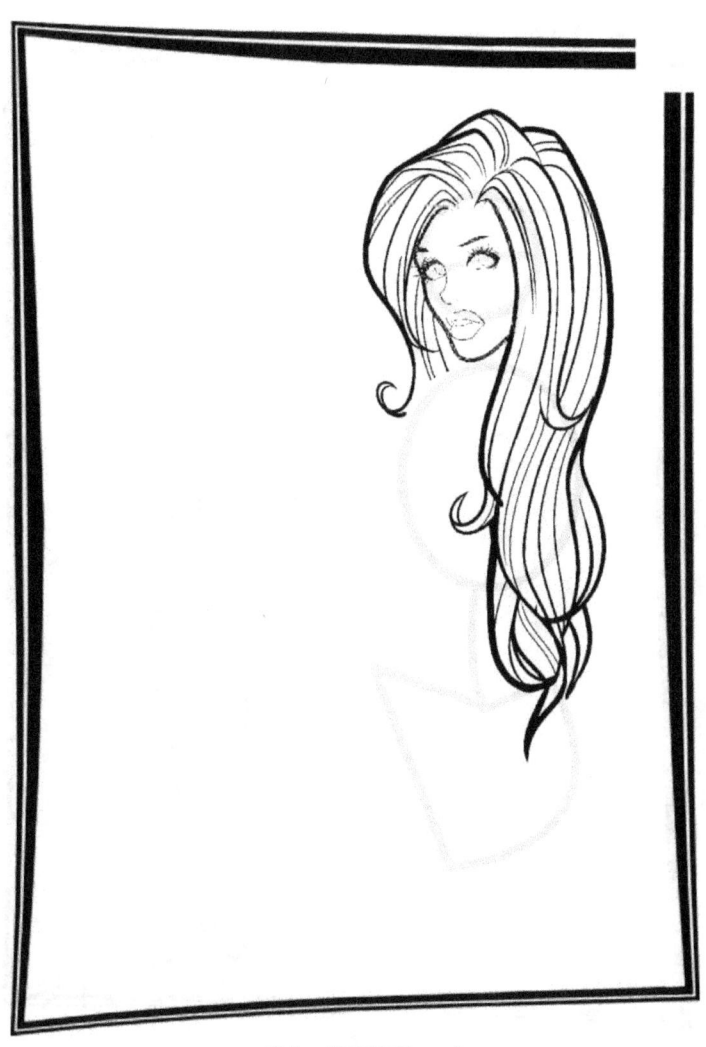

STEP 4

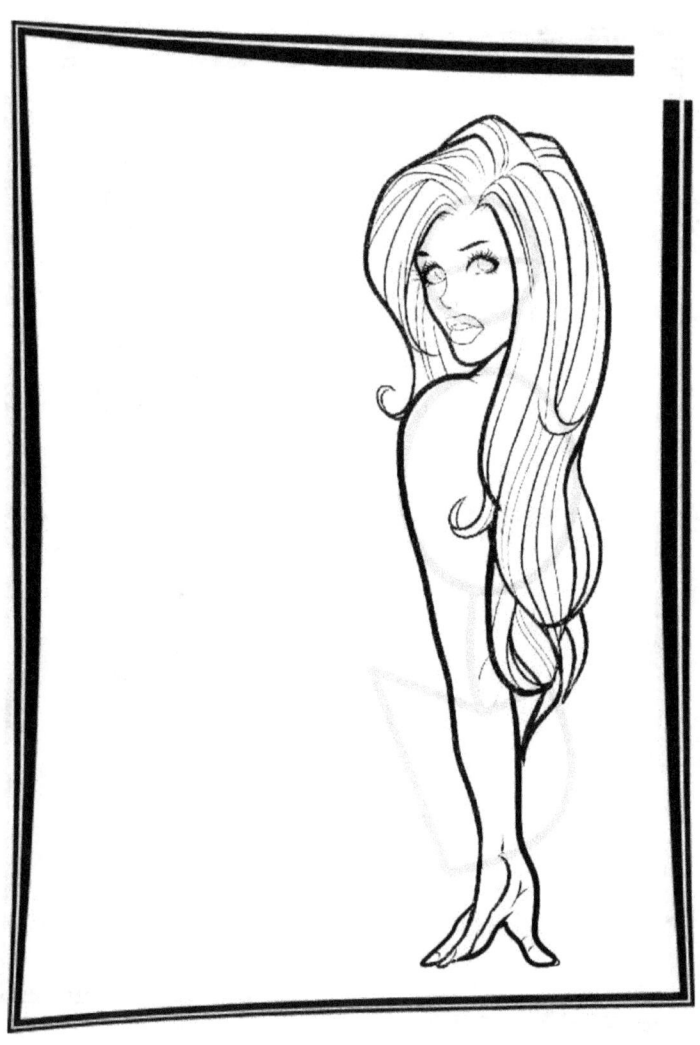

STEP 5

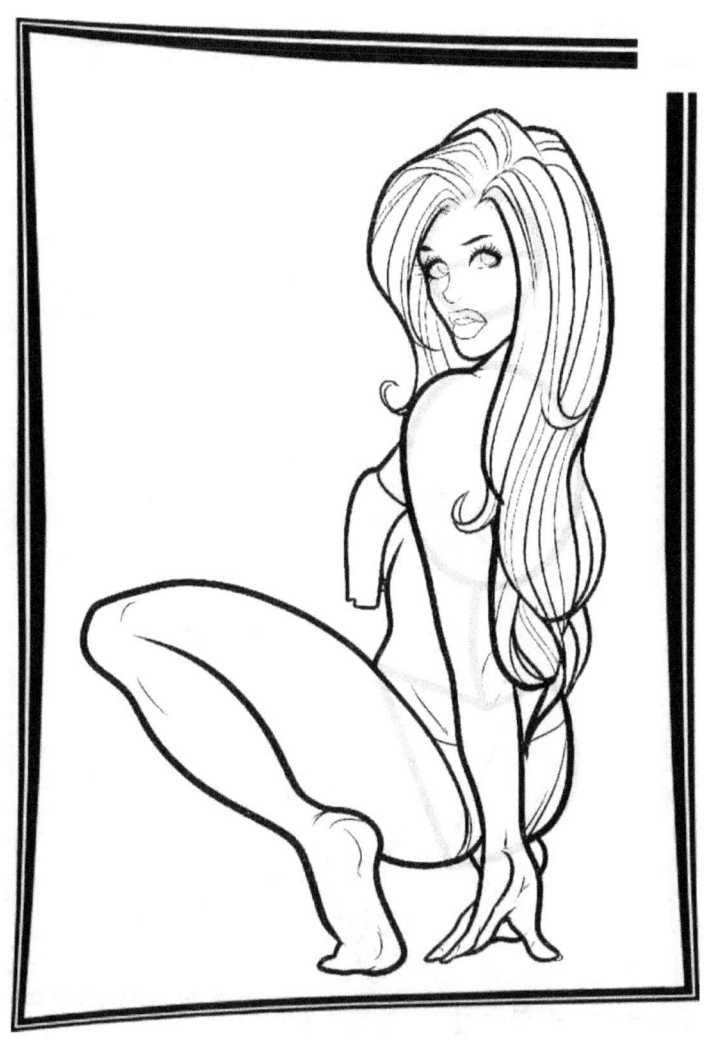

STEP 6

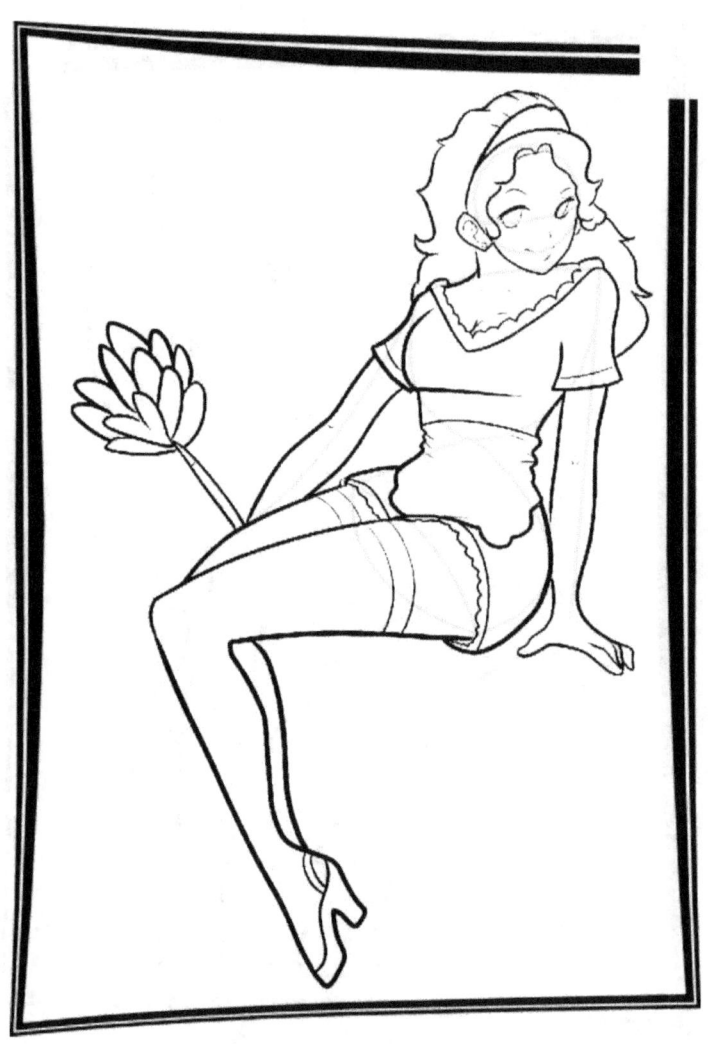

Character 3

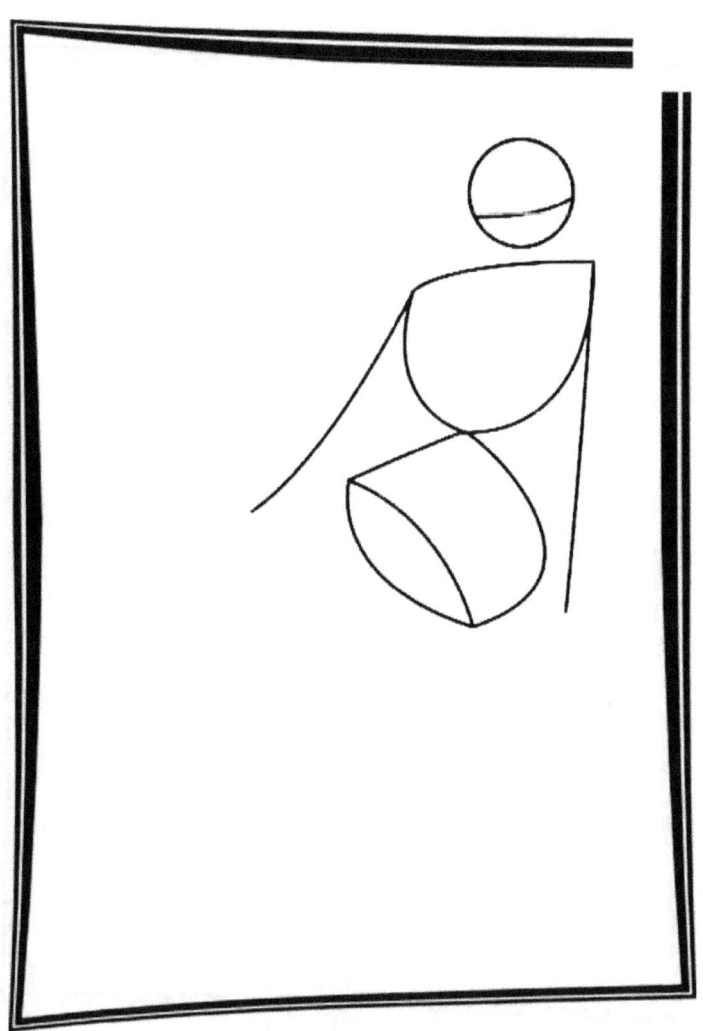

STEP 1

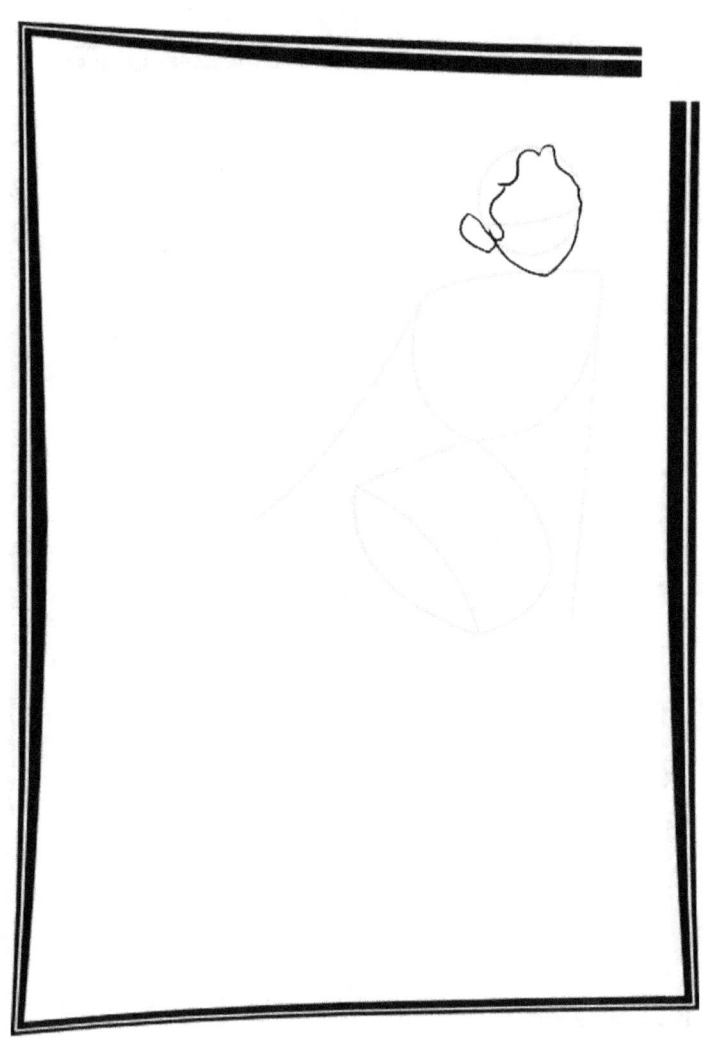

STEP 2

21

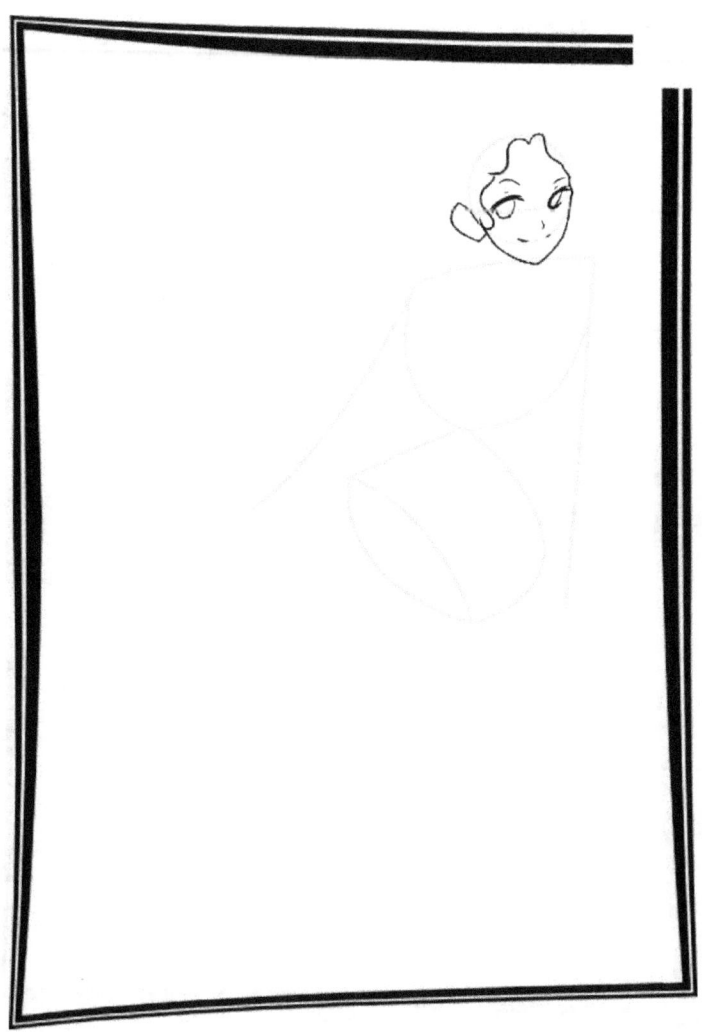

STEP 3

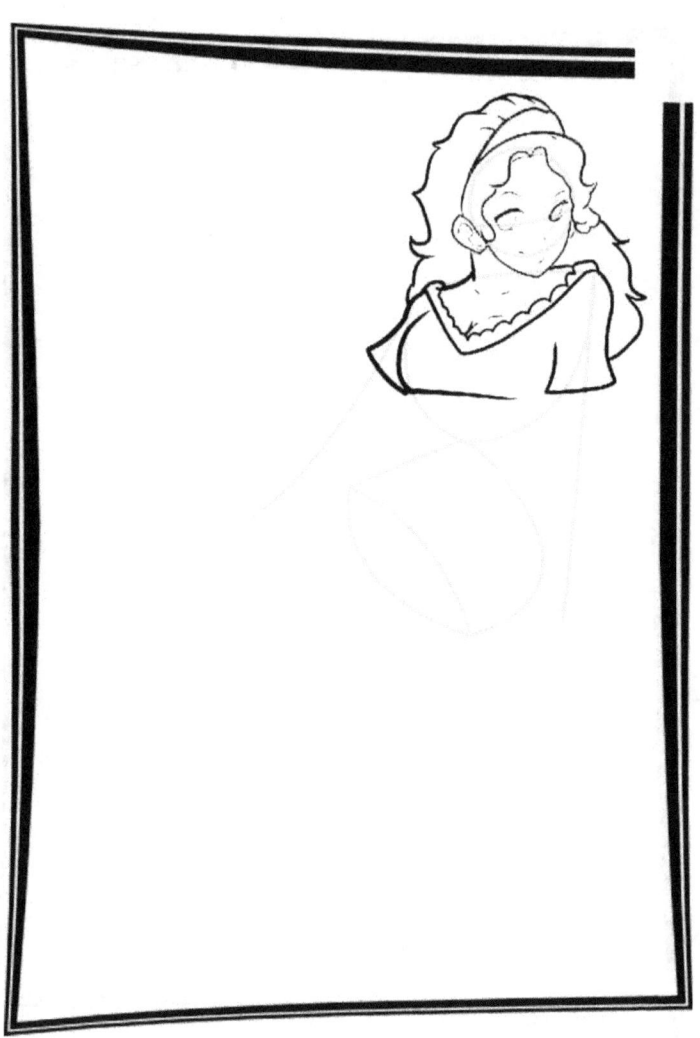

STEP 4

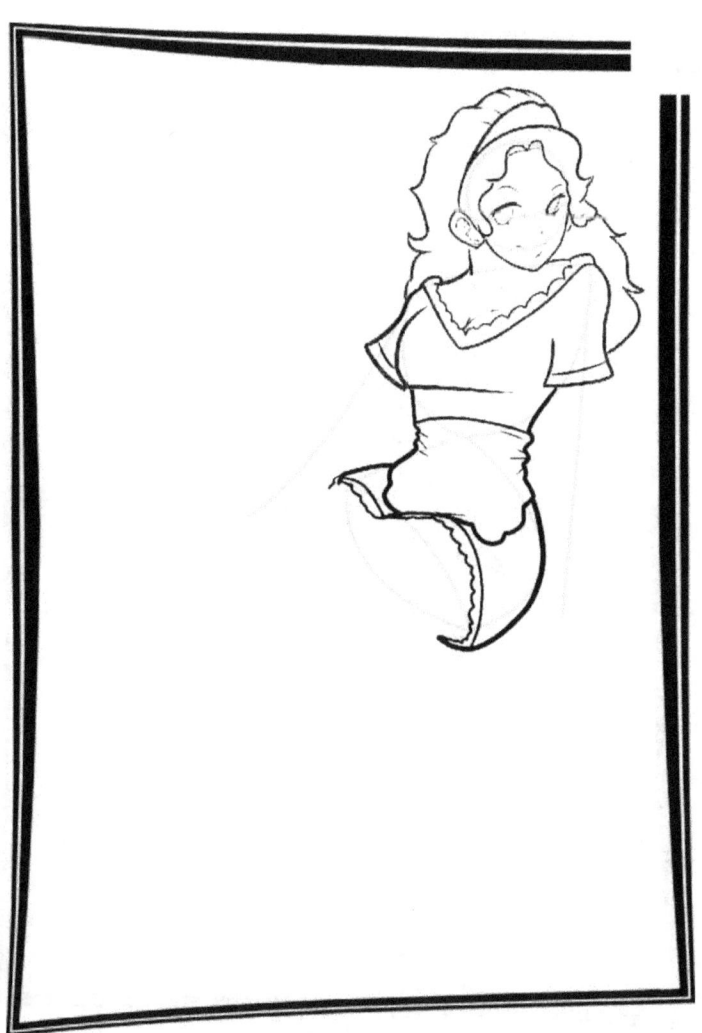

STEP 5

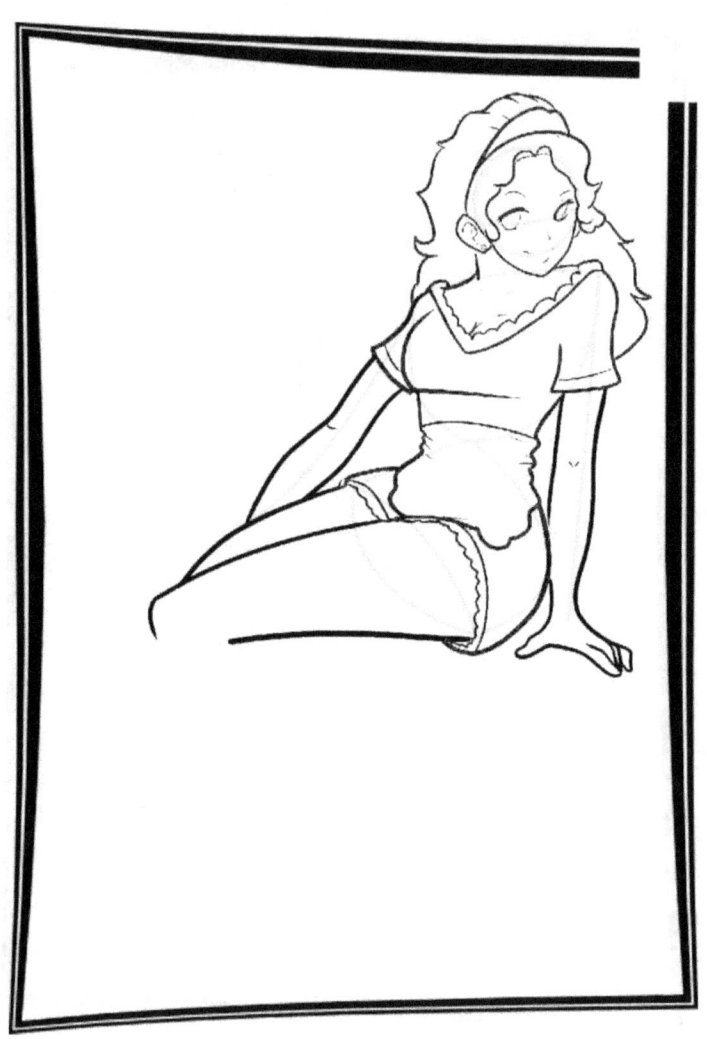

STEP 6

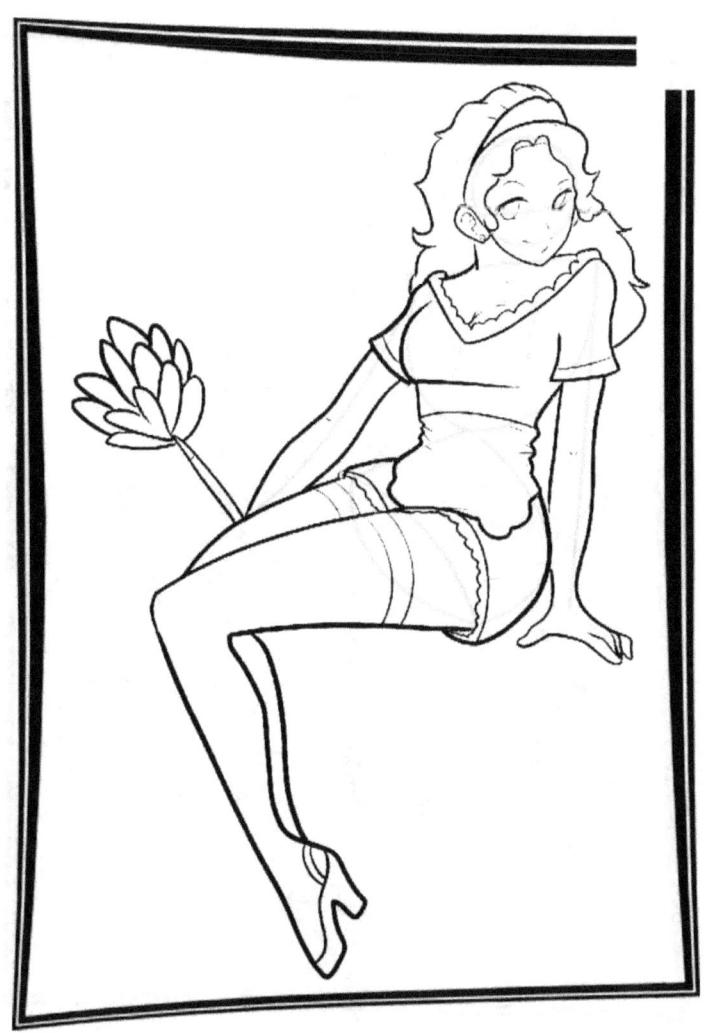

STEP 7

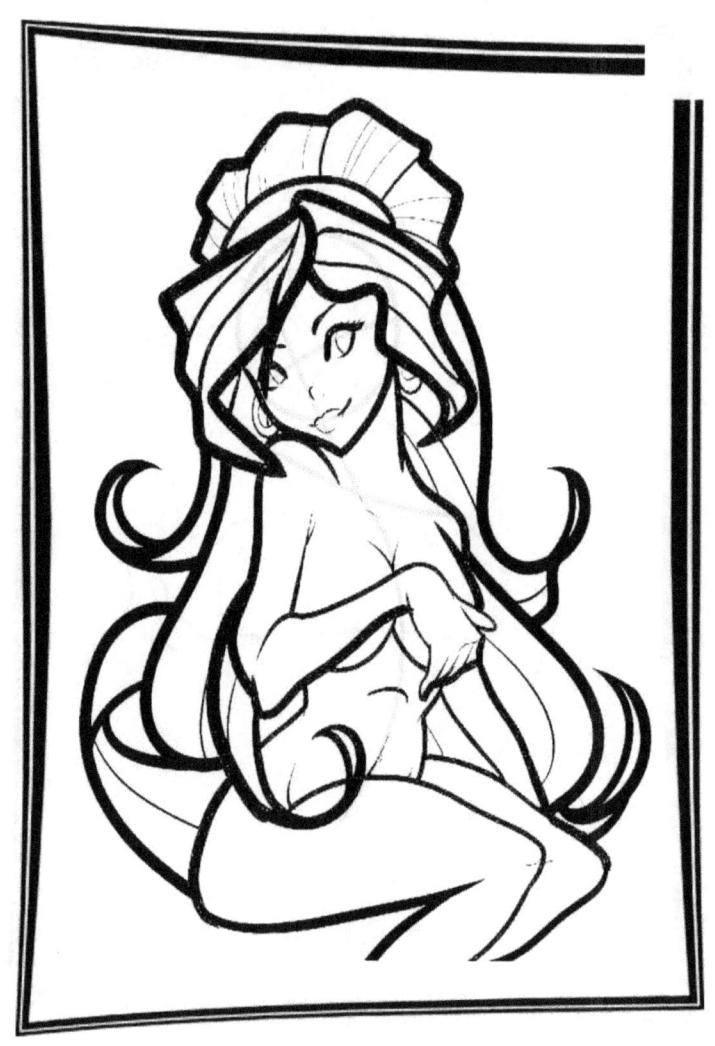

Character 4

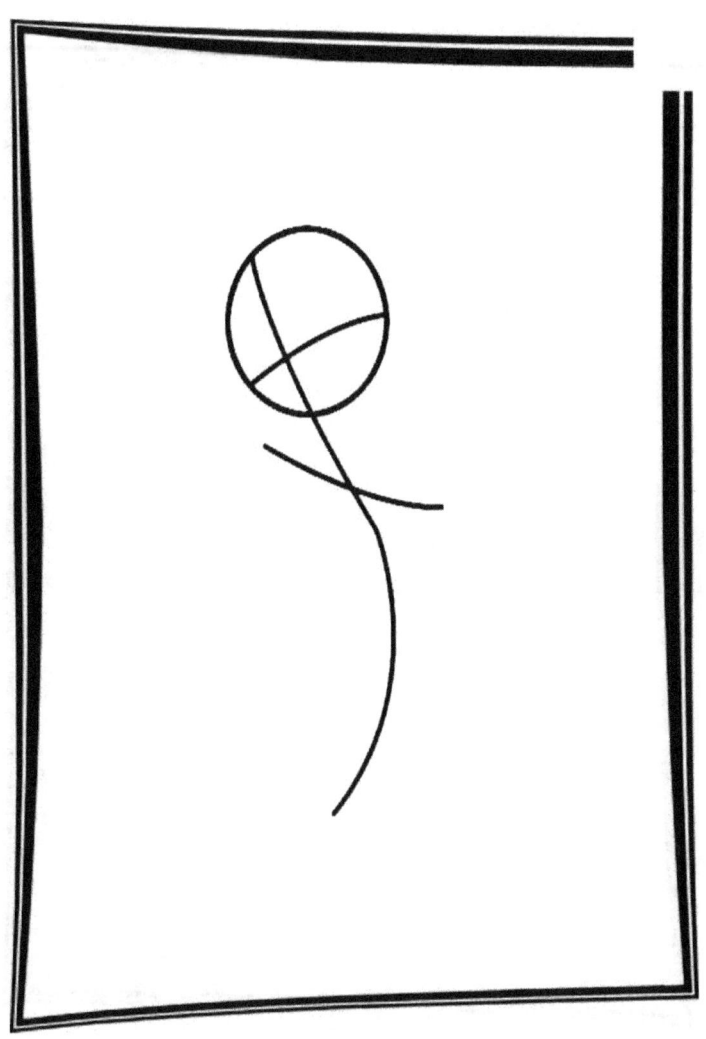

STEP 1

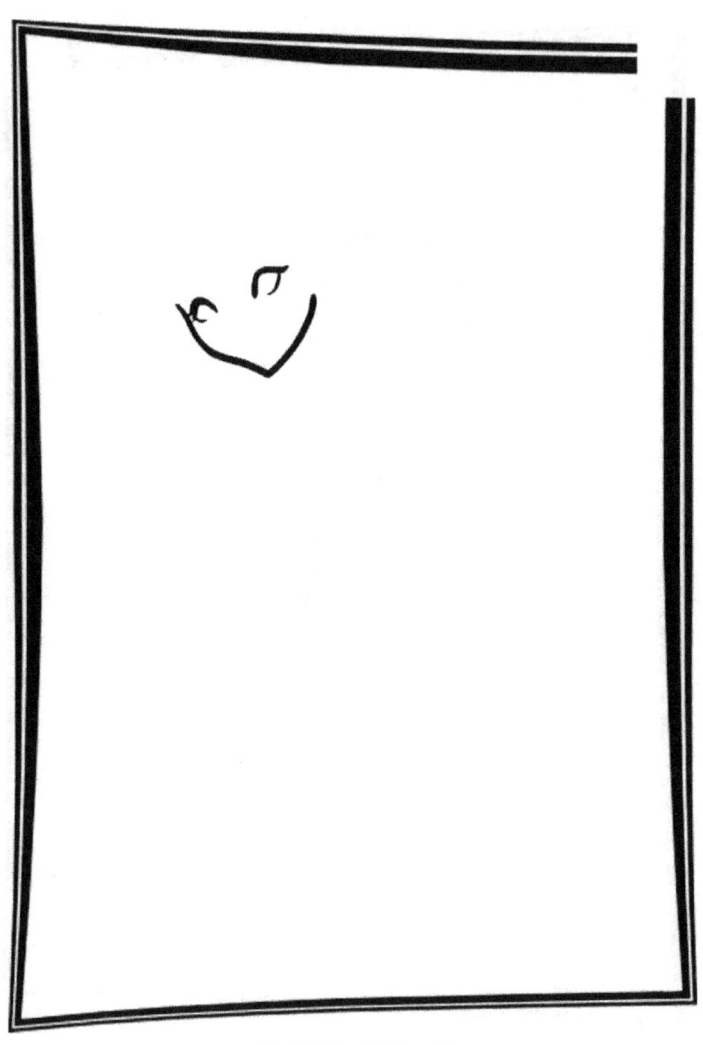

STEP 2

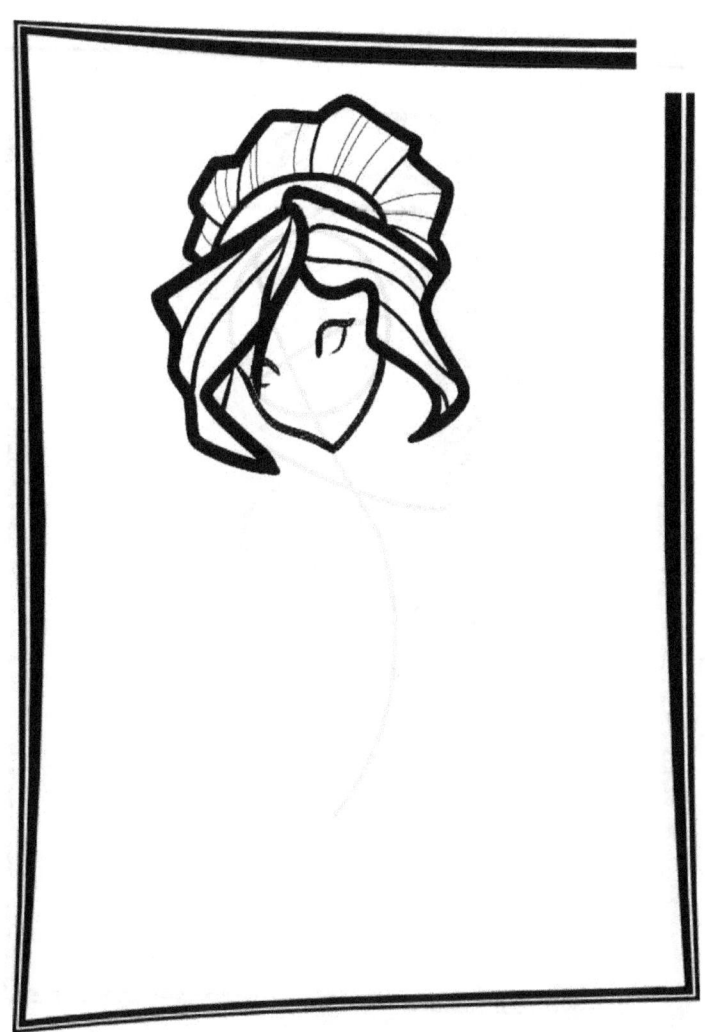

STEP 3

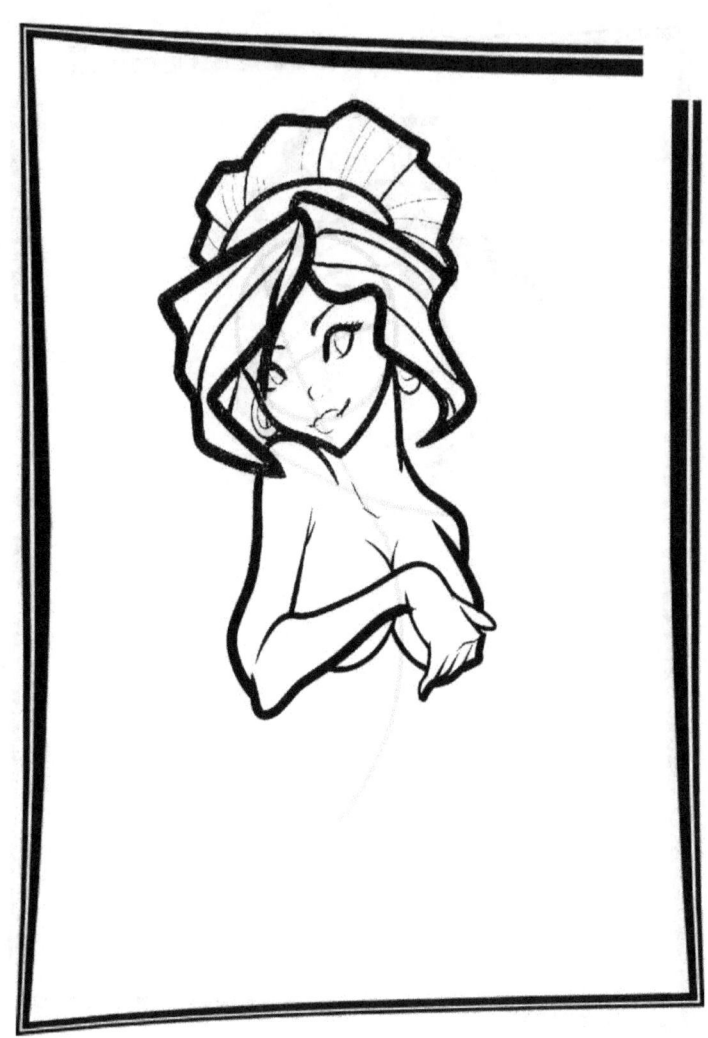

STEP 4

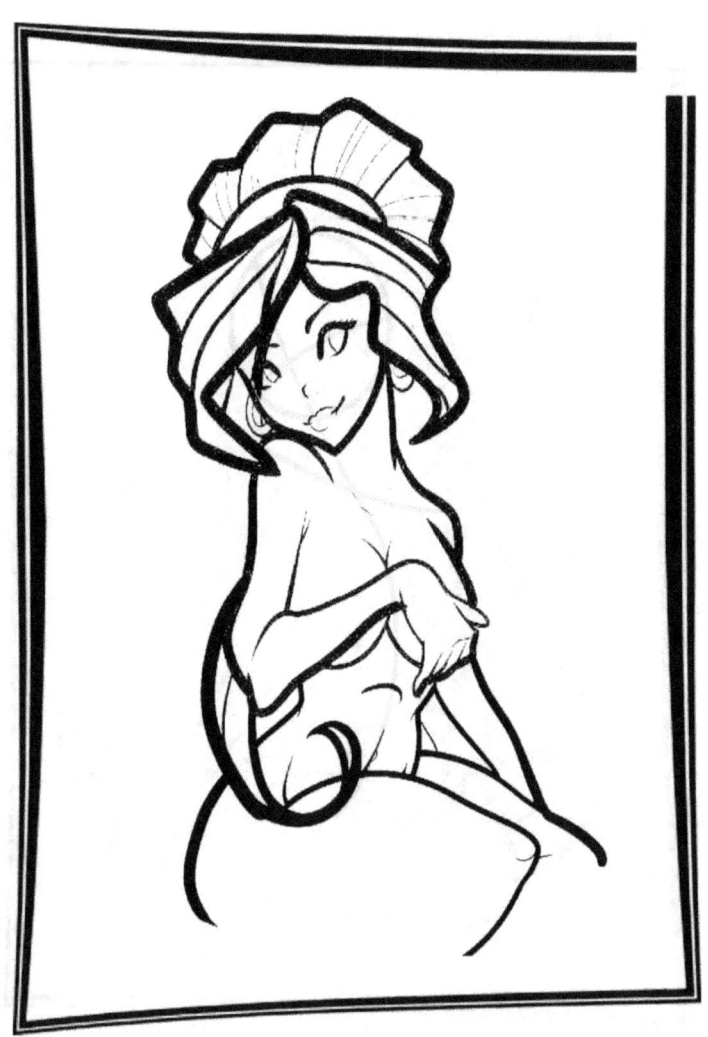

STEP 5

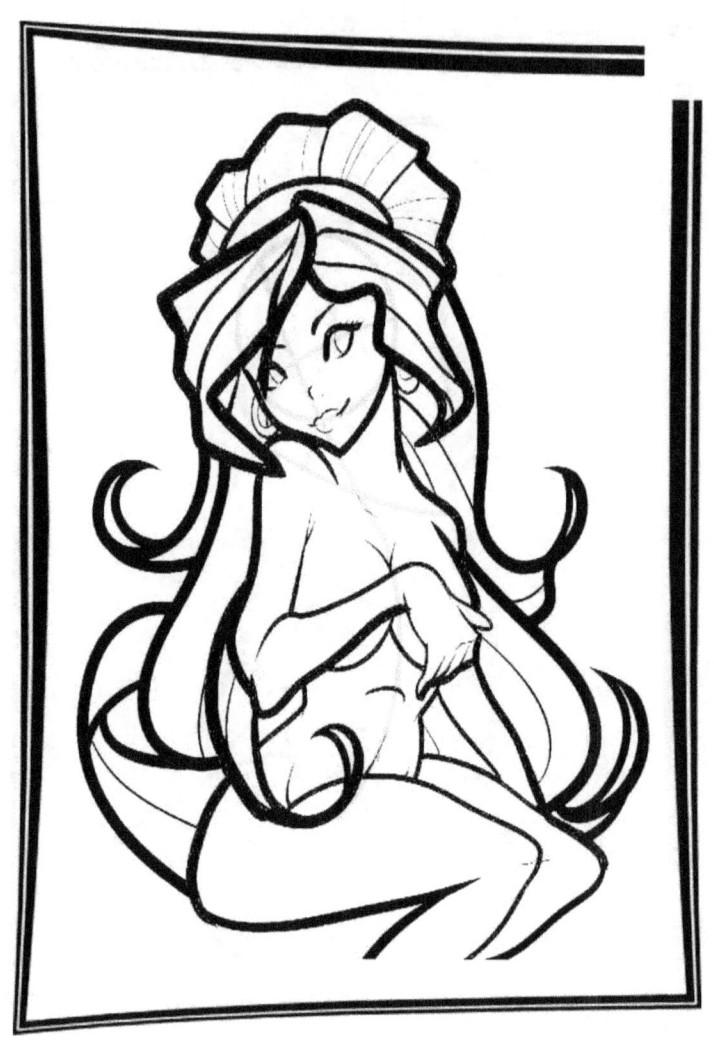

STEP 6

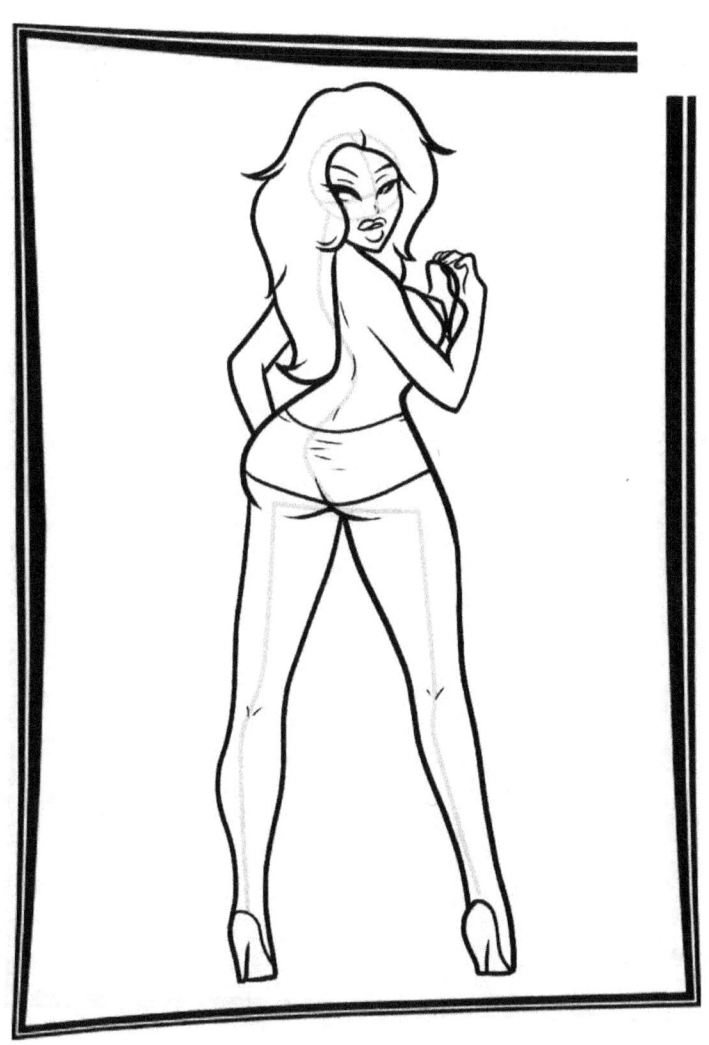

Character 5

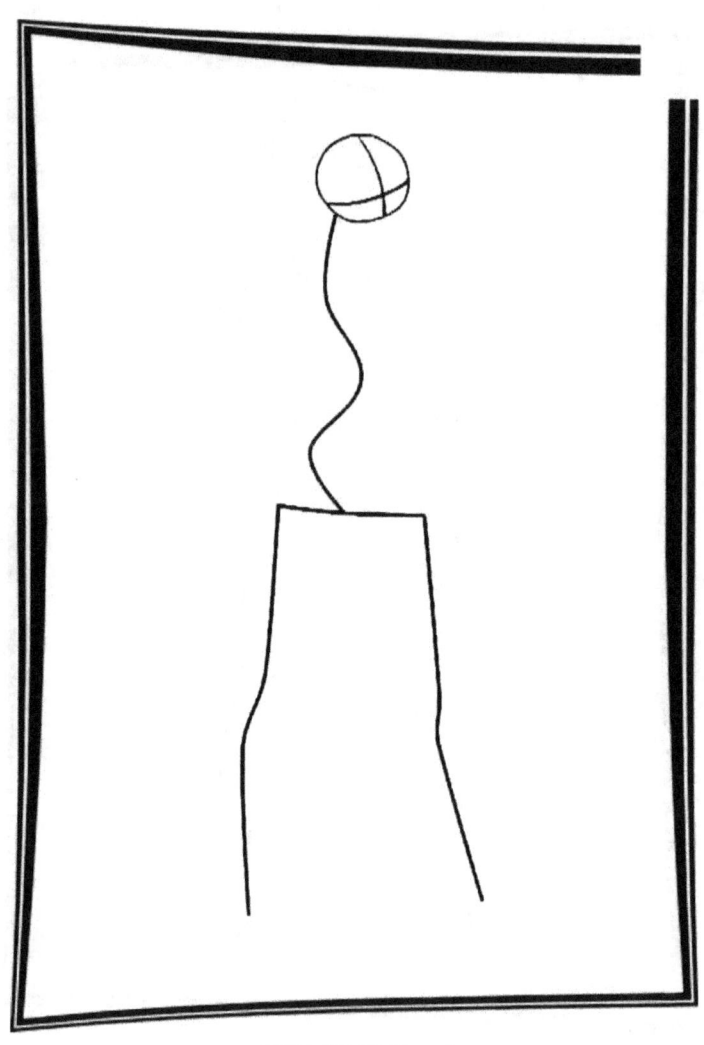

STEP 1

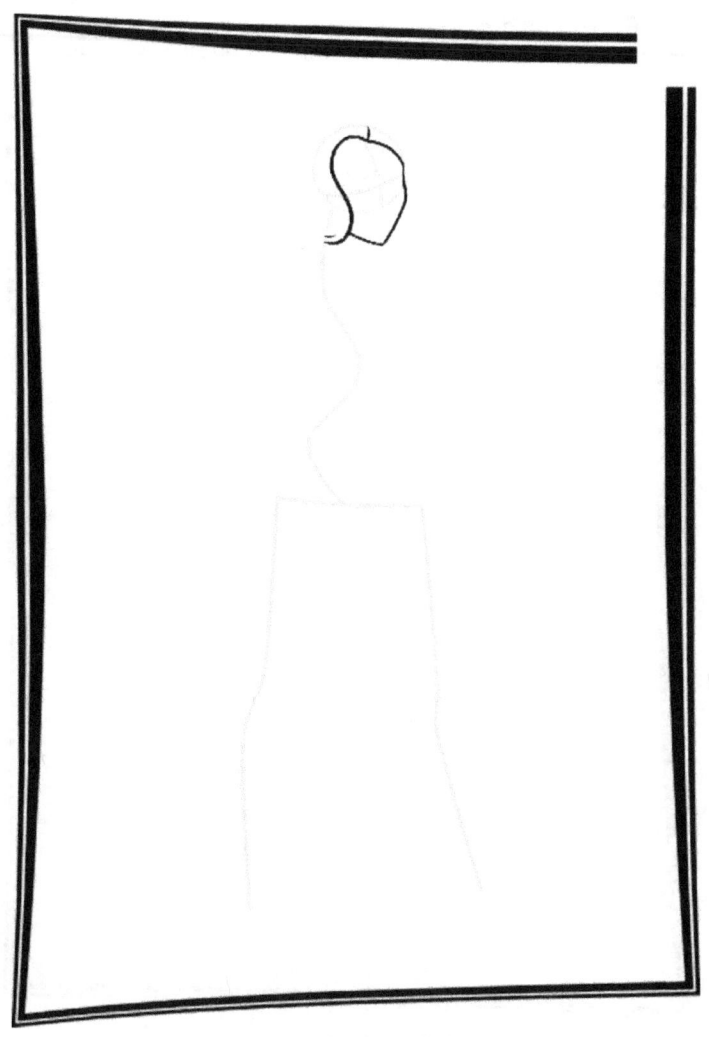

STEP 2

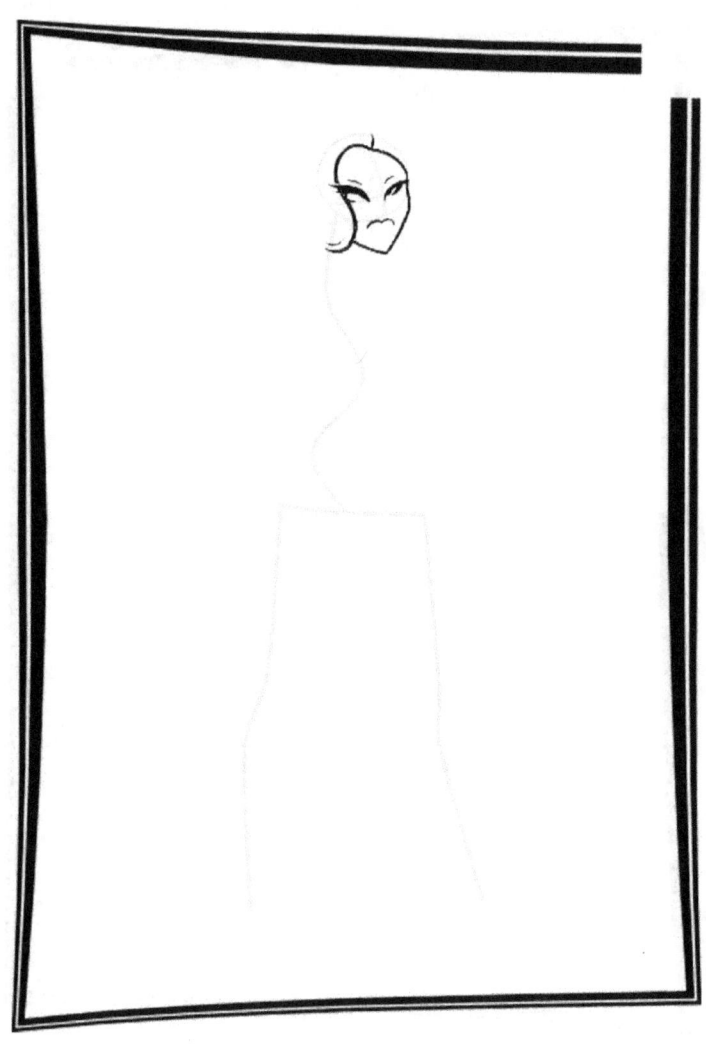

STEP 3

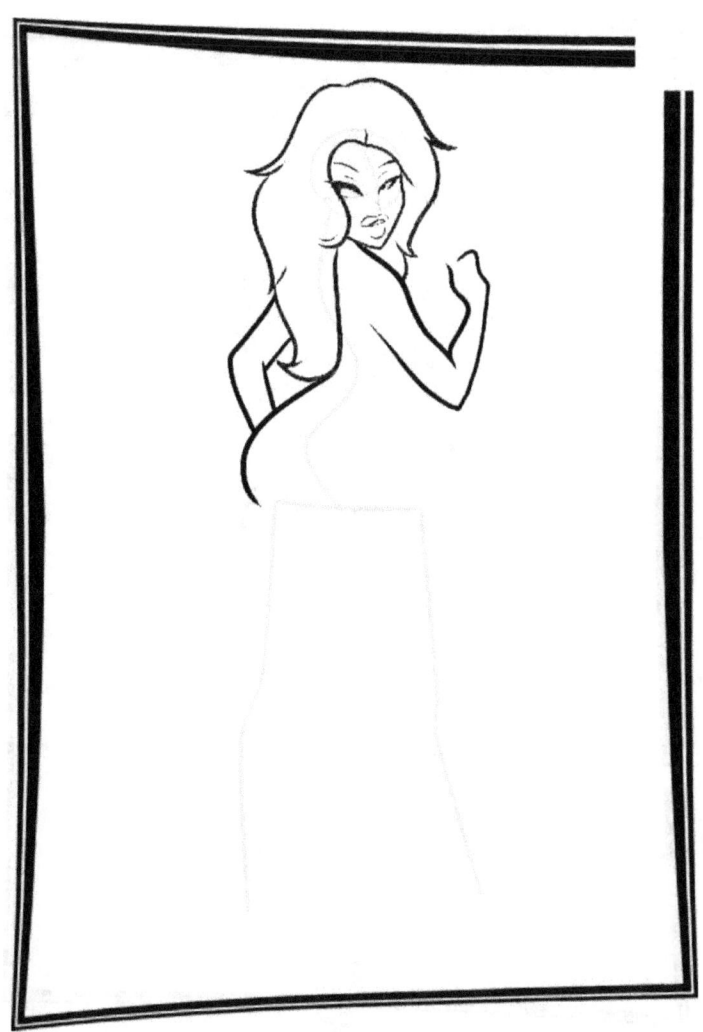

STEP 4

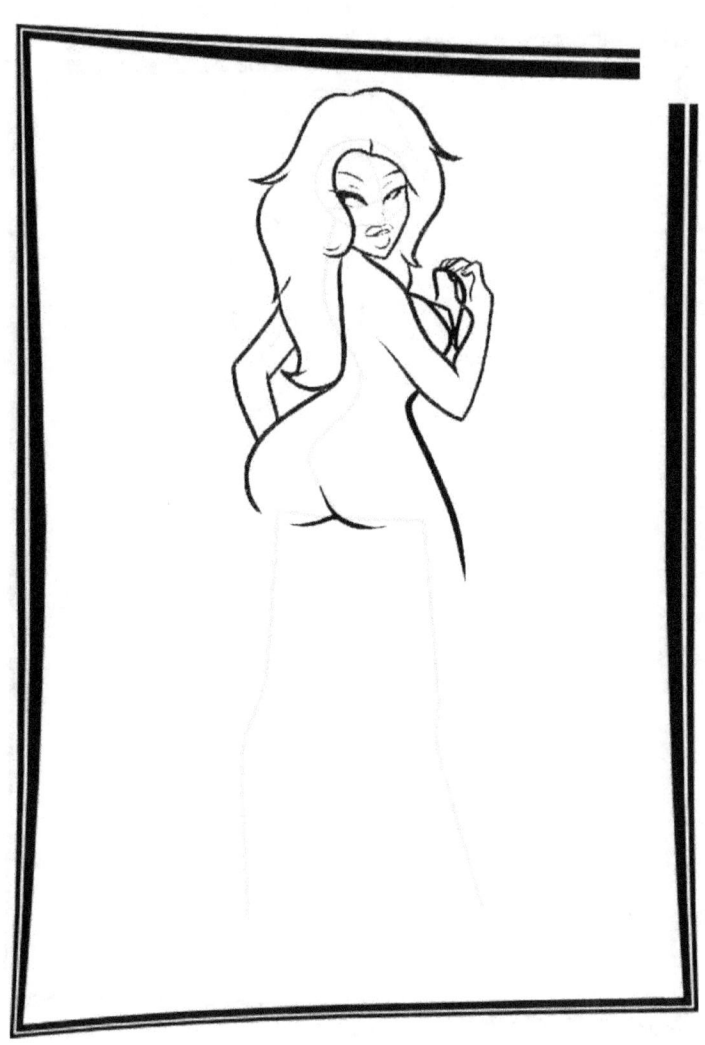

STEP 5

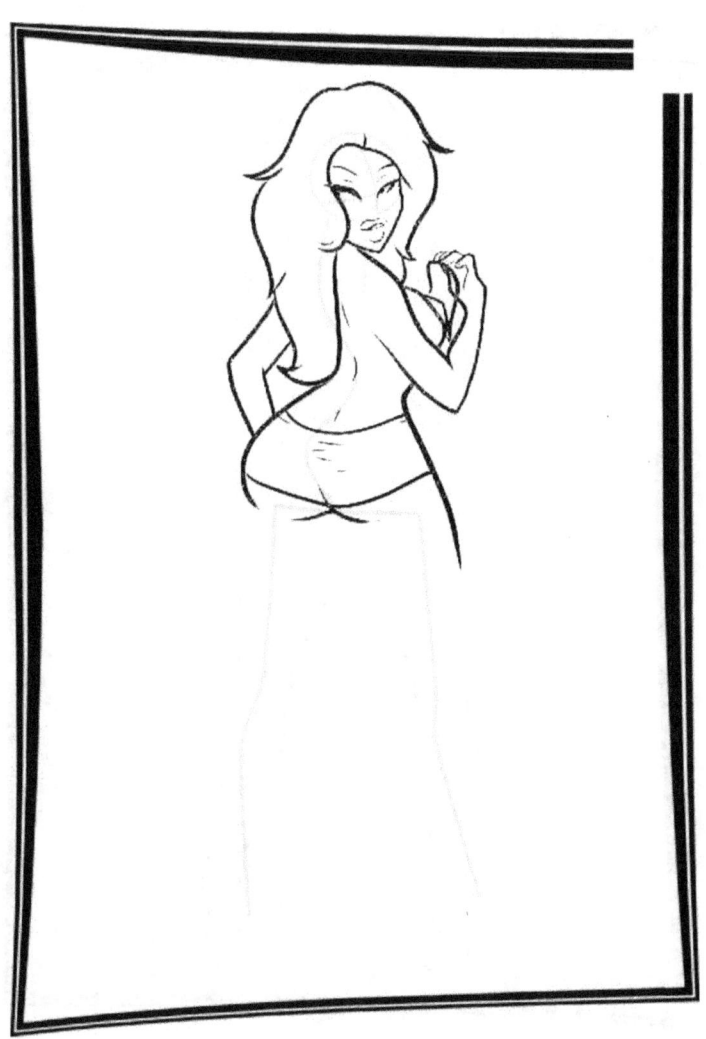

STEP 6

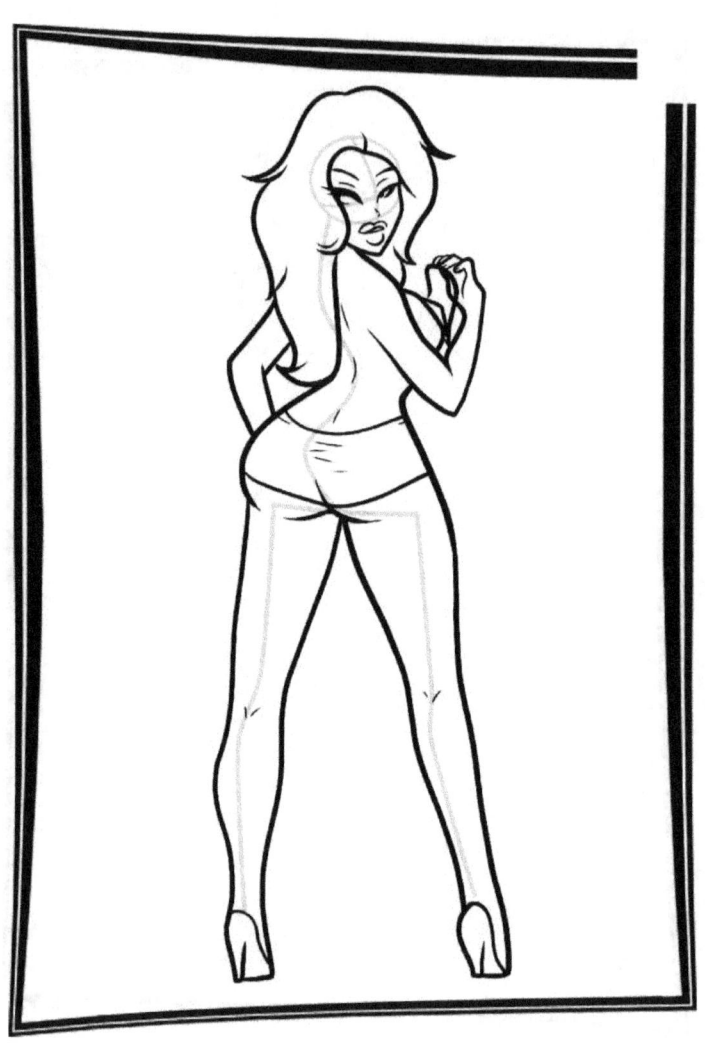

STEP 7

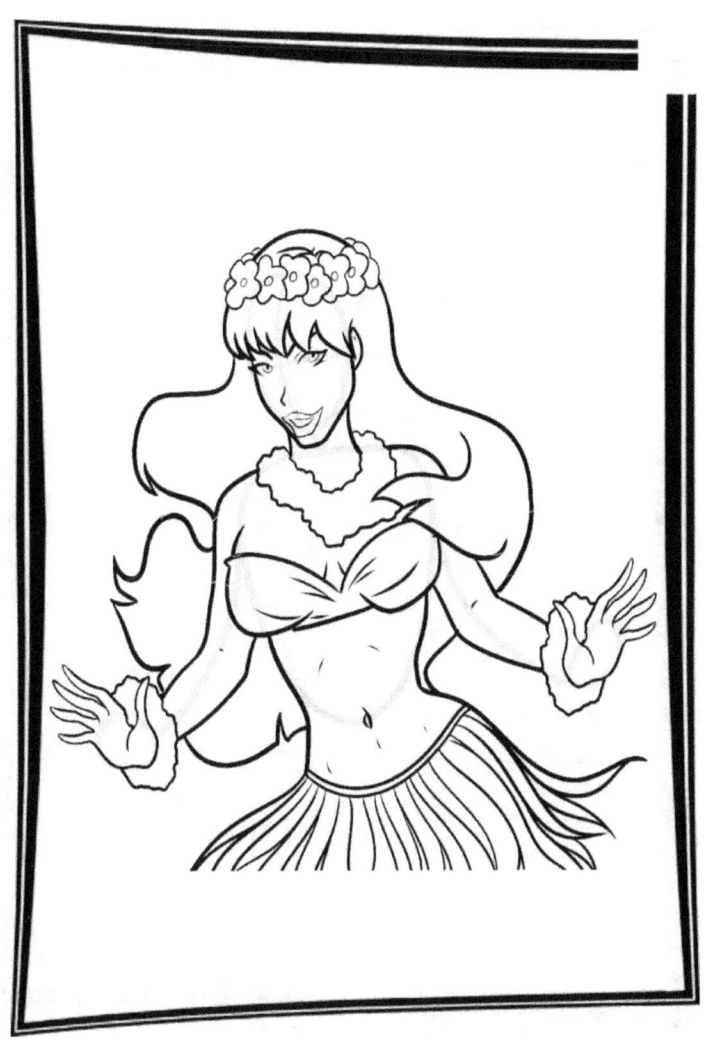

Character 6

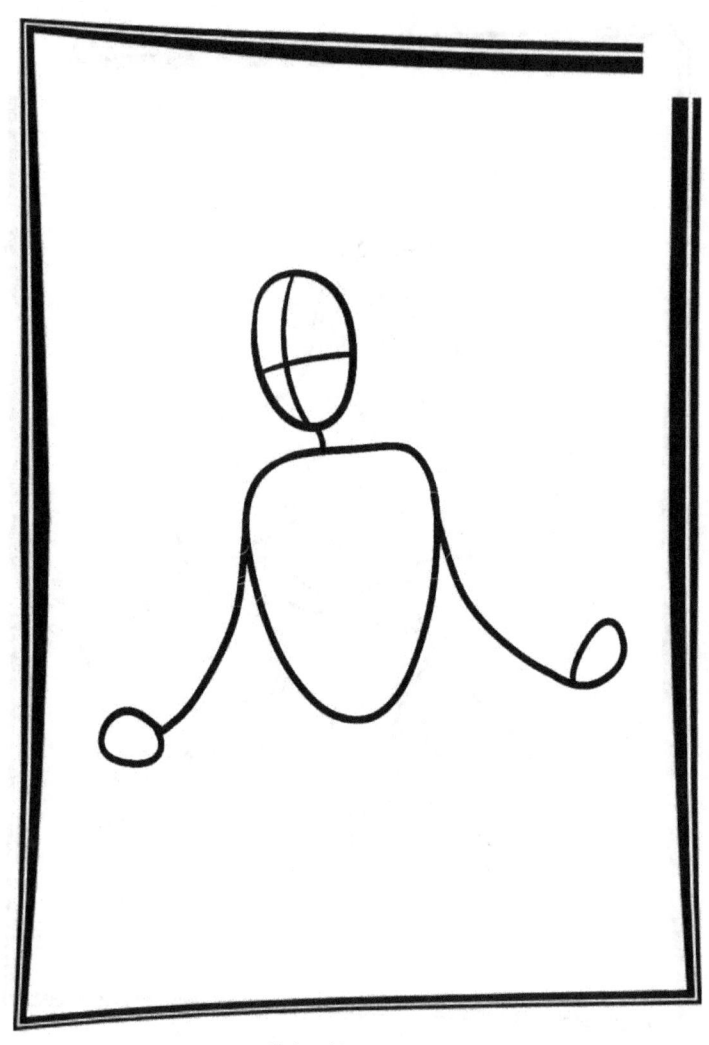

STEP 1

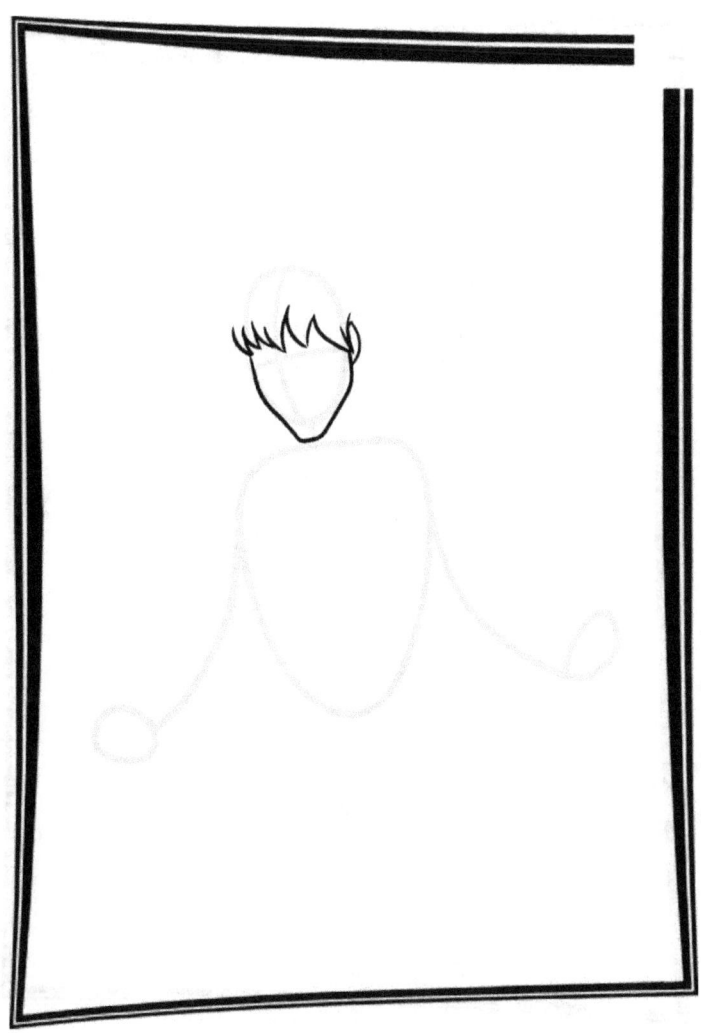

STEP 2

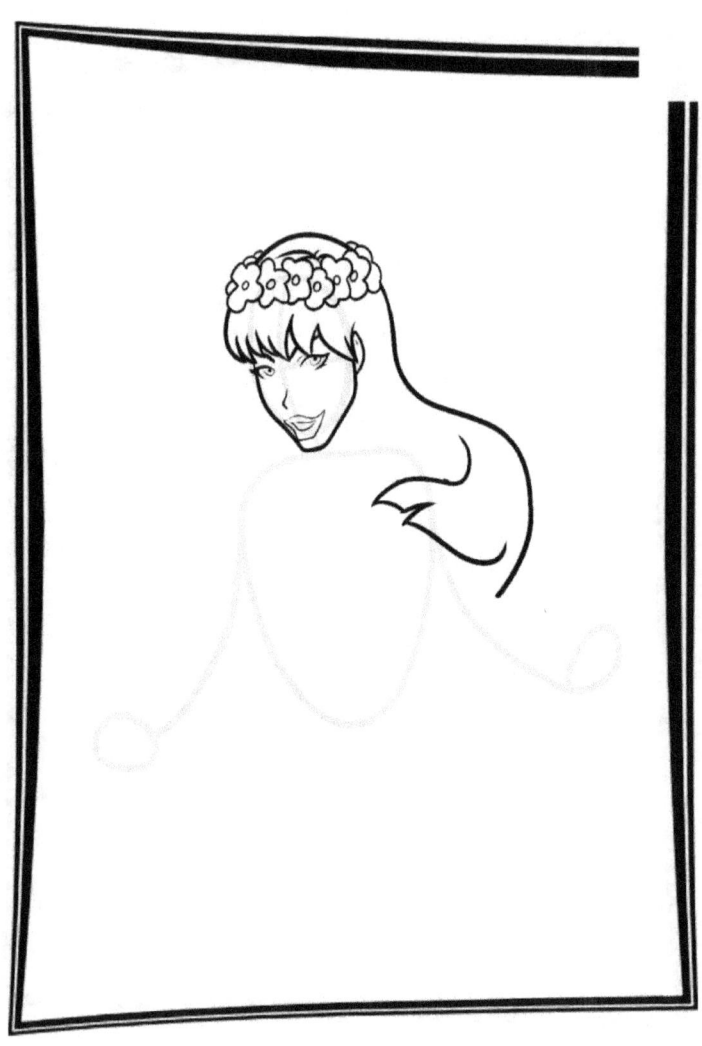

STEP 3

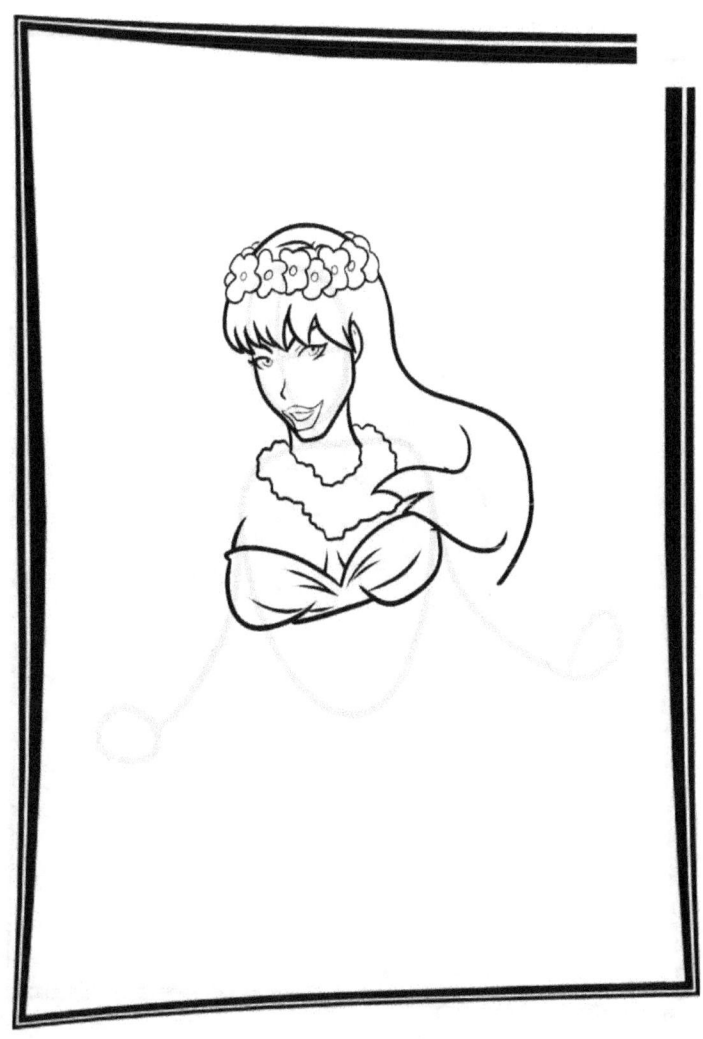

STEP 4

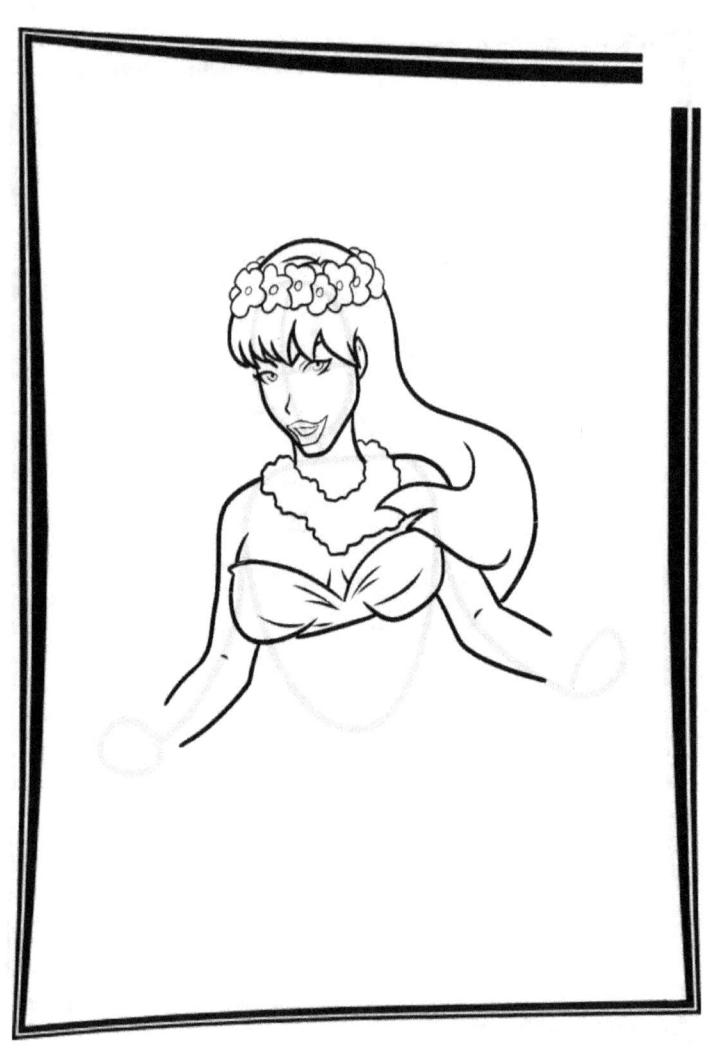

STEP 5

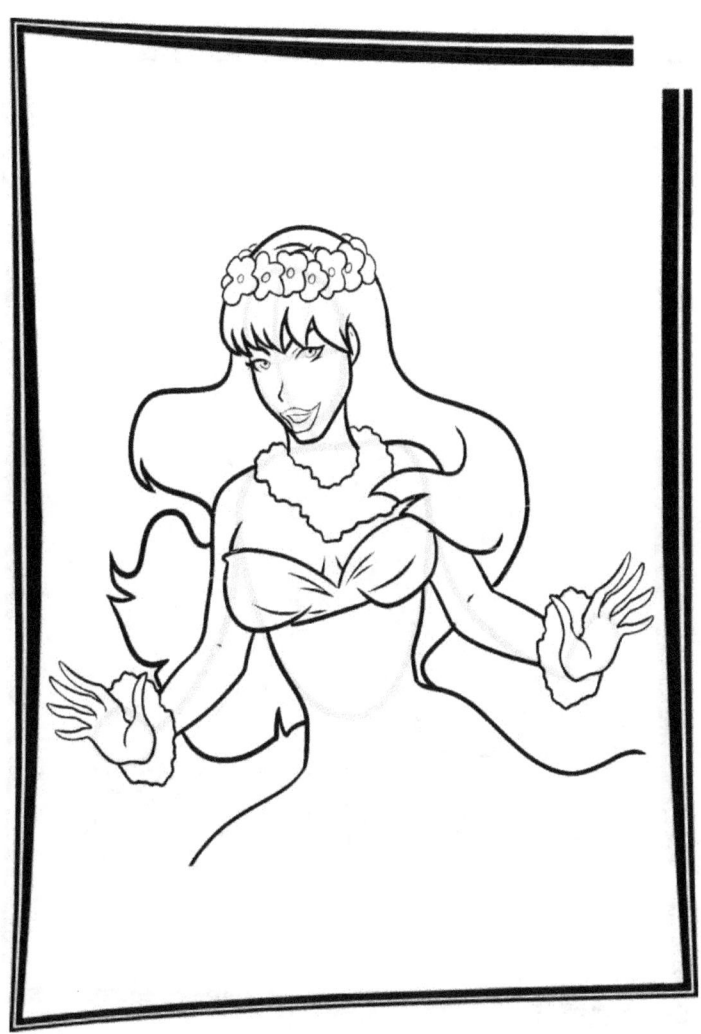

STEP 6

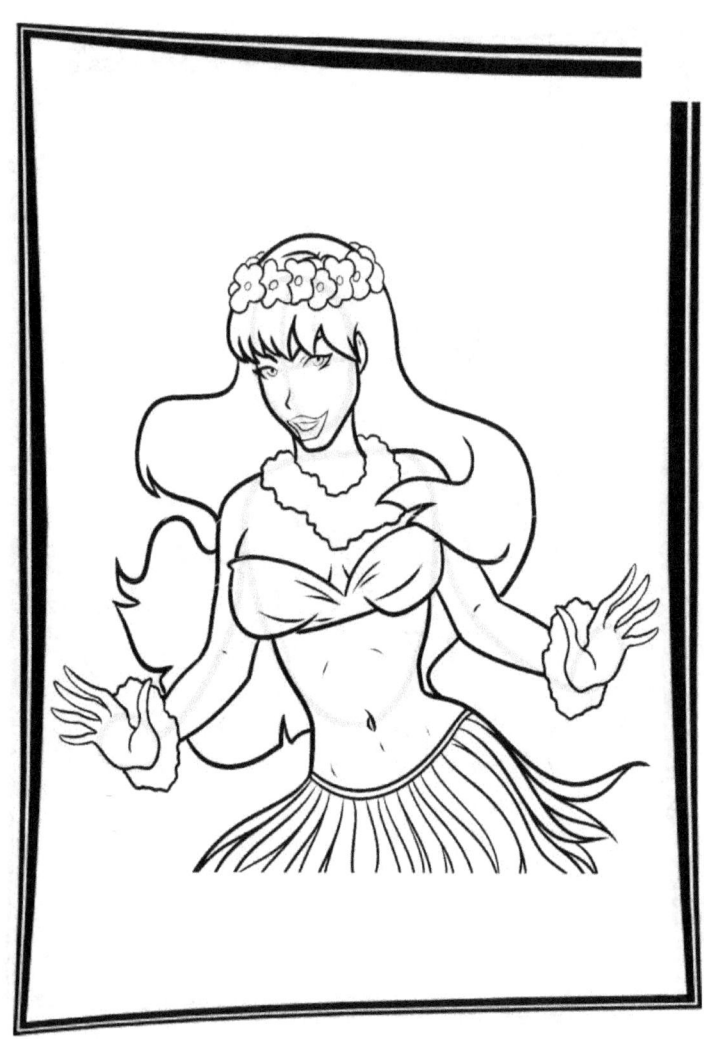

STEP 7